Snap books®

# Designer Dogs

# Puggle

## A Cross between a Pug and a Beagle

by Molly Kolpin

Consultant:
Tanya Dewey, PhD
University of Michigan Museum of Zoology
Ann Arbor, Michigan

CAPSTONE PRESS
a capstone imprint

Snap Books are published by Capstone Press,
1710 Roe Crest Drive, North Mankato, Minnesota 56003.
www.capstonepub.com

Books published by Capstone Press are manufactured with paper
containing at least 10 percent post-consumer waste.

*Library of Congress Cataloging-in-Publication Data*
Kolpin, Molly.
  Puggle : a cross between a pug and a beagle / by Molly Kolpin.
    p. cm. — (Snap. designer dogs)
Includes bibliographical references and index.
  Summary: "Describes Puggles, their characteristics and behavior, and includes basic information on feeding, grooming, training, and
health care"—Provided by publisher.
  ISBN 978-1-4296-7665-6 (library binding)
1. Puggle—Juvenile literature. I. Title.
SF429.P92K65 2012
636.753'7—dc23                                    2011036953

**Editorial Credits**
**Editor:** Lori Shores
**Designer:** Veronica Correia
**Media Researcher:** Marcie Spence
**Photo Stylist:** Sarah Schuette
**Studio Scheduler:** Marcy Morin
**Production Specialist:** Kathy McColley

**Photo Credits:**
Capstone Studio: Karon Dubke, cover (top), 5, 7, 13, 14, 15, 16, 17, 18, 21, 22, 23, 25, 27, 28, 29
Shutterstock: Eric Isselee, cover (left), 8 (left), FotoJagodka, cover (right), 8 (right), 11, Jesse Kunerth, 9

Printed in the United States of America in North Mankato, Minnesota.
102011        006405CGS12

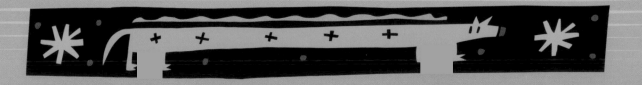

# Table of Contents

# One Cute Designer Dog

With wrinkly foreheads and floppy ears, Puggles are adorable dogs. Even better, they're lively and fun. Don't be surprised to see a Puggle chasing a ball or exploring in the yard. Whatever the task, the Puggle will tackle it with enthusiasm. The Puggle's happy, upbeat nature makes it a great family pet. Many people love this affectionate, fun-loving dog.

No one knows when the first Puggle was born. But Wallace Havens of Kingston, Wisconsin, is responsible for bringing the breed to fame. Havens began breeding Puggles in 1992 and came up with the name. He registered Puggles with the American Canine Hybrid Club (ACHC), a registry specifically for mixed-breed dogs. Today the Puggle is a well-known member of the ACHC.

# WHAT IS A DESIGNER DOG?

Designer dogs are a cross between two different **purebred** dogs. They're not purebreds, but they're not mutts, either. Mutts are unplanned combinations of different dog types, while designer dogs are purposely bred.

People began breeding designer dogs in the 1980s, often to serve a particular need. The Labradoodle, a mix of a Labrador Retriever and Poodle, is a good example. It was bred to be a good guide dog, like the Lab, but with the Poodle's shed-free coat. The breeder hoped Labradoodles would be better for people with allergies.

Today there are many kinds of designer dogs. Some, like the Labradoodle, are bred to be **hypoallergenic**. Others are bred to participate in agility competitions. Some breeders hope to reduce the chance of passing on health issues common to purebred parents. But Puggles, like many other designer dogs, are bred simply to be good pets.

**purebred**—having parents of the same breed

**hypoallergenic**—possessing a quality that reduces or eliminates allergic reactions

# Not for the AKC

The American Kennel Club (AKC) is an organization that keeps track of dogs' pedigrees. This group sponsors events such as the Westminster Dog Show. The AKC registers only purebred dogs. Purebred breeds must have consistent traits. Designer dogs, however, often look quite different from one another. For this reason, the AKC does not recognize designer dogs as pure breeds.

Jack-A-Bees are a mix of Jack Russell Terrier and Beagle.

# Chapter 2

# Puggle Parents

Getting to know a designer dog means learning about its parents. For Puggles, this means looking at the Pug and Beagle.

Beagle

Pug

Pugs were originally loyal, faithful pets for members of the Chinese royalty. With their sweet, loving natures, these dogs bond closely with people. Most Pugs seem to enjoy snuggling on a warm lap.

Pugs are known for their wrinkly faces and bodies. They have thick, stocky bodies and tightly curled tails. One of the smallest breeds, Pugs are part of the toy group. Like other toy breeds, they have short legs. Their short, soft coats are black or fawn-colored with black ears and a black mask on their face.

With their little legs, Pugs tire easily. Many Pugs also have breathing problems that can make exercise difficult. For these reasons, Pugs are not good pets for active people. But for people looking for a calm companion, Pugs are delightful pets.

# BOLD BEAGLES

While Pugs like to relax, Beagles are all about action and adventure. Beagles came from England, where they were used to hunt hares. Today they still have a strong hunting **instinct**. Like other dogs in the hound group, Beagles have a powerful sense of smell. Even well-trained Beagles struggle to obey their owners when tempted to follow a scent.

Long, floppy ears and big, brown eyes make Beagles easily recognizable. They are slightly larger than Pugs. Beagles have thick coats that are usually a mix of black, white, and tan colors. Most Beagles also have dark saddle markings on their backs.

Beagles make excellent pets for active owners. They are good playmates for children. But those hoping for a calm, quiet dog should look elsewhere. Beagles are full of life and have energy and enthusiasm to spare.

instinct—behavior that is natural rather than learned

# Beware of Puppy Mills!

Pugs and Beagles are popular dogs, but sometimes popularity has a downside. Puppy mills breed as many puppies as possible without providing proper care to the dogs. Always be sure you're not dealing with a puppy mill. Visit the breeder and ask to see where the dogs are kept. If it does not seem clean or big enough to house the animals comfortably, it could be a puppy mill.

# Chapter 3
# The Best of Both Worlds

The Puggle is a great combination of its parents. In many ways, Pug and Beagle **traits** balance out in the Puggle. The Beagle side makes the Puggle more active than a Pug. But the Pug side gives the Puggle a calmer **temperament** than that of a Beagle. The Puggle is equally happy exploring open spaces or relaxing quietly indoors.

Of course, not all Puggles are the same. Some Puggles behave more like Pugs. Others act more like Beagles. Sometimes the situation determines which side takes over. When outdoors, the Puggle's Beagle curiosity often comes out. Owners must keep an eye on their Puggle so it doesn't wander off. Indoors, however, Puggles like to stick with their owners. Like Pugs, they are companion dogs that form close bonds with their human family.

trait—a quality or characteristic that makes one person or animal different from another

temperament—the combination of an animal's behavior and personality

13

Puggles are mid-sized dogs. Most stand 10 to 15 inches (25 to 38 centimeters) tall. They weigh 15 to 30 pounds (7 to 14 kilograms). They have short, smooth fur. Some have black coats. Other coats are multi-colored with black and tan, or black, tan, and white markings. But most Puggles are fawn-colored with black masks on their faces, like Pugs.

Puggles get their wrinkly foreheads and curled tails from their Pug side. But their long, floppy ears are definitely from the Beagle. Usually the Puggle's **muzzle** looks more like a Beagle's. But some Puggles may have short, wrinkly muzzles like a Pug.

## Dog Fact!

Breeders may produce toy puggles by breeding pugs with smaller beagles. Toy puggles are about 10 pounds (4.5 kg) lighter than standard puggles. Some call these smaller dogs "pocket puggles."

muzzle—an animal's nose, mouth, and jaws

# Chapter 4

# Caring for a Puggle

Like all pets, Puggles require time and attention. Having a dog is a big responsibility. But properly caring for a Puggle is well worth it. Healthy, well-behaved dogs make wonderful pets.

# TRAINING

Puggles are naturally sweet-tempered and loving dogs. But even a friendly dog needs training. Be prepared to house-train your Puggle first. It can be challenging, but a puppy needs to learn where you expect it to go potty. Next, basic commands, such as sit, stay, and come, are good first choices for behavior training.

Keep training sessions short for Puggles. Dogs have limited attention spans and can't focus for long. Puggles, like all dogs, learn best when they're in a positive environment. Never show that you're frustrated or your dog may become frustrated as well. And don't forget to reward your Puggle for a job well done. Small treats help Puggles to learn during training.

# FEEDING

A regular feeding schedule is important for Puggles and other dogs. Like their parents, Puggles can easily become overweight. These dogs are known to eat beyond their needs. Plus, with their excellent sense of smell, it's easy for Puggles to sniff out a snack. Your veterinarian can help you choose a high-quality dog food. Be sure to measure out your Puggle's meals according to the package recommendations. And always have fresh water available for your Puggle.

# No-No Foods!

Dogs have a way of begging that is hard to resist. But it is best for dogs to stick with their own food. Some "people foods" can make your dog sick. Keep these foods away from your dog.

- grapes and raisins
- plums
- macadamia nuts
- peaches
- milk products
- chocolate

# EXERCISE

Some Puggles are more active than others, but all dogs need exercise. Many Puggles get enough exercise by playing in the house or yard. A fence will keep your Puggle from getting lost chasing after a rabbit or a squirrel.

Puggles also enjoy a 15 to 30 minute walk each day. Even dogs that don't need a lot of exercise will benefit from a walk. Dogs have a strong instinct to walk with their **pack**. And who wouldn't be bored cooped up in the house all day?

Another great exercise for a Puggle is playing fetch or Frisbee. Many dogs love to chase after a ball. And some dogs can be trained to catch a Frisbee in their mouths. The great thing about playtime is that you'll both get exercise and some good bonding time.

**pack**—a small group of animals that hunts together

# GROOMING

All dogs need grooming. While Puggles do not have long coats, they must still be brushed at least once each week. They also need their teeth brushed daily. Puggles should be bathed once a month with dog shampoo. Take special care to wash the folds of skin so they don't get irritated. After bathing, an adult should trim the Puggle's nails with clippers made for pets.

# VISITING THE VET

Puggles are generally healthy. Some have eye or knee problems, but these are rare. Like all dogs, Puggles need regular check-ups and **vaccinations**. It's also important to have your Puggle spayed or neutered. This operation prevents some types of cancer and keeps your dog from having puppies.

vaccination—a shot of medicine that protects animals from a disease

# Chapter 5

# Adopting a Puggle

Puggles are a popular family pet. But every family is different, and so is every Puggle. Before adopting a Puggle, think about what you want in a pet. What energy level and personality traits will fit best with your family?

All dogs need owners who will take care of their needs. Puggles do well in homes with family members who will play with them. They also enjoy getting out of the house to explore new areas. Like other dogs, Puggles need regular routines and feeding schedules. And while Puggles don't need much grooming, they still need special care to ensure good health.

# Should You Adopt a Puggle?

Answer the following questions. If you answer mostly "no," the Puggle probably isn't for you.

1. Are you home enough to spend time with a dog?
2. Do you have a yard where a dog can run and play?
3. Are you patient enough to train a dog?
4. Do you have time to walk a dog every day?
5. Will you keep a regular feeding schedule?

# PICKING A PUGGLE

If you decide to adopt a Puggle, try an animal shelter first. Because Puggles are popular, they might be hard to find. But even purebreds and designer dogs sometimes end up at shelters. If there are no Puggles at your local shelter, check other shelters online. A quick search will help you find animal shelters in your area.

## Mutts Are Good Pets Too!

You'll probably meet many dogs at the animal shelter. Not all will be purebreds or designer dogs, but they can still make great pets. If the Puggle isn't right for you, consider choosing a shelter dog. Read up on the breeds that make up a mixed breed dog you like. Learn what kinds of behaviors to expect from mixed breeds. Then you can make a responsible decision about which dog is right for you.

27

If you can't find a Puggle at a shelter, you can look for a breeder. Good breeders raise dogs that are happy, healthy, and well cared for. Ask about the Puggles' parents. Healthy parents usually mean the puppies will be healthy too. When it comes time to select your Puggle, closely watch how the puppies act. Do you want a calm Puggle or a playful one? Take your time to choose the best dog for you.

Caring for a Puggle is a big job. But with big jobs come big rewards. Although every Puggle is different, owners can count on one thing. For all the effort put into your Puggle, you'll be paid back in endless love and companionship.

# Glossary

**agility** (uh-GI-luh-tee)—the ability to move in a quick and easy way; many owners train their dogs to participate in agility competitions

**hypoallergenic** (hye-poh-a-luhr-JEN-ik)—possessing a quality that reduces or eliminates allergic reactions

**instinct** (IN-stingkt)—behavior that is natural rather than learned

**muzzle** (MUHZ-uhl)—an animal's nose, mouth, and jaws

**pack** (PAK)—a small group of animals that hunts together; dogs consider their human family to be their pack

**pedigree** (PED-uh-gree)—a list of an animal's ancestors

**purebred** (PYOOR-bred)—having parents of the same breed

**temperament** (TEM-pur-uh-muhnt)—the combination of an animal's behavior and personality; the way an animal usually acts or responds to situations shows its temperament

**trait** (TRATE)—a quality or characteristic that makes one person or animal different from another

**vaccination** (vak-suh-NAY-shun)—a shot of medicine that protects animals from a disease

# Read More

**Gagne, Tammy.** *Beagles.* All about Dogs. Mankato, Minn.: Capstone Press, 2010.

**Landau, Elaine.** *Pugs Are the Best!* The Best Dogs Ever. Minneapolis: Lerner Publications Co., 2011.

**Wheeler, Jill C.** *Puggles.* Dogs. Edina, Minn.: ABDO Pub., 2008.

# Internet Sites

FactHound offers a safe, fun way to find Internet sites related to this book. All of the sites on FactHound have been researched by our staff.

Here's all you do:

Visit *www.facthound.com*

Type in this code: 9781429676656

# Index